# Another Jar of Tiny Stars

Poems by More NCTE Award-Winning Poets
Children Select Their Favorite Poems

**EXPANDED EDITION**

**BERNICE E. CULLINAN**
AND
**DEBORAH WOOTEN, EDITORS**

PORTRAITS BY MARC NADEL

WORDSONG

NATIONAL COUNCIL OF TEACHERS OF ENGLISH
HONESDALE, PENNSYLVANIA

Wordsong
An Imprint of Boyds Mills Press, Inc.
815 Church Street
Honesdale, Pennsylvania 18431
Printed in the United States of America

Library of Congress Cataloging-in-Publication Data

Another jar of tiny stars : poems by more NCTE award-winning poets /
Bernice E. Cullinan and Deborah Wooten, editors ; portraits by Marc Nadel.
— Expanded ed.
p. cm.
Includes bibliographical references and index.
ISBN 978-1-59078-726-7 (hardcover : alk. paper)
1. Children's poetry, American. I. Cullinan, Bernice E. II. Wooten, Deborah.
III. Nadel, Marc, ill. IV. National Council of Teachers of English.
PS586.3.A56 2009
811.008'09282—dc22
2009017131

First edition
The text of this book is set in 13-point Adobe Caslon.
The portraits are done in watercolor washes.

10 9 8 7 6 5 4 3 2 1

# Acknowledgments

A special thanks goes to the following teachers:

Marty Abbendandelo, Glenwood Landing
Susanne H. Alford, The Pingry School
Lucille Allaire, Clover Street School
Allen, Fairfax Elementary
Jill Allen, South Knoxville Elementary
Kay Allison, Barbour Elementary School
Cindy Hobby Ammons, Ritta Elementary
Mrs. Ammons, Karns Elementary
Kathleen Armstrong, Mary Institute and
    St. Louis Country Day School
Sophia Ash, South Greenville Elementary
Kristie Atwood, Webb School
Belinda Avery, Brentwood Elementary
Carla Avery, Fairglen Elementary School
Gerry Bain-Ryder, Glenwood Landing
Caroline Baker, Webb Lower School
Gwen Barrett, Russell School
Laura Barton, Webb Lower School
Erin Baulch, Glenwood Landing
Beth Beach, John Harshaw School
Karen Beard, Vineyards Elementary School
Faye Beauchanys, Kingston Elementary
Nancee Beidler-Torns, Anna Reynolds School
Christie Beittel, Fern Bluff Elementary
Amelia Bell, Glenwood Elementary
Cindy Bender, Mary Institute and
    St. Louis Country Day School
Theresa M. Benedetti, Bryant School
Heidi Bennett, Galindo Elementary
Tanya Best, Lanier Elementary
Bev Blumberg, Loomis School
Tahra McKeever Boatright, Brentwood Elementary
Ally Boehlow, Mary Institute and
    St. Louis Country Day School
Ashley Booher, Ritta Elementary
Lauren Boucher, South Greenville Elementary
Ruth Bowers, Fairglen Elementary School
Mrs. Bowers, Karns Elementary
Sue Bradin, Fairglen Elementary School
Kristin Braig, Rose Tree Elementary School
Ellen Brand, William Yates Elementary
Mrs. Brantley, Karns Elementary
Elaine Braus, Springdale School
Dennis Brock, Copper Ridge Elementary
Dr. Amy Broemmel, University of Tennessee
Luella Brown, Northwest Middle
K. Buckshaw, Holbrook School

Nathan Bugg, Parrottsville Elementary
Kelly Bunn, East Carolina University
Diana Burger, Wetherill School
Mrs. Byrd, Karns Elementary
Mrs. Campbell, Karns Elementary
Phoebe Cascaden, Delcroft Elementary School
Colleen Chamberlain, Green Park Elementary
Teresa Charles, South Knoxville Elementary
Carol Chastain, Eagleton Elementary
Daniel Chemnitz, Sea Cliff School
Jan Chilis, Northwest Middle
Diane Christie, Glenwood Landing
Patricia Ciotoli, Glenwood Elementary School
Mrs. Clapp, Karns Elementary
Stacey Clay, Washburn School
George Coe, Lanier Elementary
Ruth Gail Cohen, Worrall School
Yegi Cole, Halls Elementary School
Mary Conaty, Webb Lower School
Ed Conti, Guggenheim School
Elizabeth Contrell, Webb Lower School
Kim-Marie Cortez-Riggio, Glenwood Landing
Suzanne Costner, Montval Elementary
Carla Countiss, South Knoxville Elementary
Charlene Cox, Lakeview School
Donna Crasky, Rose Tree Elementary School
Denise Crawhorn, Fairview Elementary
Mrs. Creech, Karns Elementary
Heidi Criswell, Elmhurst Elementary
Kelly Crooks, Woodlyn School
Kate Curran, Mathew Elementary
Martha Dachos, Wallingford Elementary School
Sabrina Damrow, St. John Neumann Catholic
Christine Dano, Rose Tree Elementary School
Bridgette Davidson, Washburn School
Mrs. Dent, Karns Elementary
Terry Depp, Karns Elementary
Jim DeRose, Wallingford Elementary School
Lynne Dewees, Indian Lane Elementary School
Helene Dichter, Worrall School
Denise Dittrich, Pond Gap
Margaret Dooley, South Greenville Elementary
Kathleen Dorman, St. John Neumann Catholic
Lisa Dowd, Worrall School
Joyce Dowdy, The King's Academy
Patricia Downes, Mile Creek School
K. Driscoll, Luxmanor Elementary School
Melinda Drumheller, Brickey-McCloud Elementary
Mary Anne H. Dugan, Pennell Elementary School

# Acknowledgments

Mrs. Durfee, Karns Elementary
Gayle Durrance, Vineyards Elementary School
Andie Ebert, Sea Cliff School
Kathleen Edwards, Vineyards Elementary School
Michelle Egner, KAEC
Caroline P. Elliott, Kiona Benton Elementary
Mrs. Elliston, Karns Elementary
Chris Elmore, Elmhurst Elementary
Mrs. Elmore, Karns Elementary
Sandy Eshleman, Coeburn Elementary School
Adam Evans, Mavry Middle School–Jefferson County School
Gail Falkoff, P.S. 79 Queens
Mary Falls, Park Lane Elementary School
Kristy Faulkner, Barton Hills Elementary
Fillman, Fairfax Elementary
Carol Flamini, Culbertson Elementary School
Twila Forster, The King's Academy
Susan Fournier, Main Street School
Rosemary Fowler, Coeburn Elementary School
Sonya Freeman, Porter Elementary
Dawn French, Mary Institute and St. Louis Country Day School
Sandy Fuchs, Porter Elementary
Cindy Fugate, Maynardville Elementary
Heather Garbarino, Tioga Elementary School
Mary S. Gaynor, Ivy Drive School
Jack Geiser, Brentwood Elementary
Anthony Gervase, Barbour Elementary School
Bobbie Gettis, Pennell Elementary School
Ashley Geyer, Chicago International Academy
Heather Giancola, Springdale School
Johanna Gilbert, Coker Creek Elementary
Dr. Colleen Gilrane, University of Tennessee
Diane Ginn, Columbus School
Liz Goodstone, Glenwood Landing
Shirley Graham, Latimer Lane School
Grass, Kingston Elementary
Ms. Graves, Pond Gap
Margie Gray, Fern Bluff Elementary
Lena Green, Fairfax Elementary
Becky Greene, South Knoxville Elementary
C. Greene, Kingston Elementary
Debbie Greene, Winship School
Rhonda Greer, Vineyards Elementary School
Andrea Gresko, Donnelly Elementary School
Kelli Grewell, Nightengale Elementary
Rebecca Griffing, Harry L. Johnson Elementary School
Mr. Grimac, Karns Elementary
Heidi Gross, Havertown, PA
Wendy Guidotti, Glenwood Landing
Mrs. Gump, Karns Elementary
Sandra Hall, Kingston Elementary
Harris, Oak Ridge Alternative School

Claudia Harris, Elmhurst Elementary
Peggy Harrison, Wickliffe School
Greg Hathcock, Porter Elementary
Greg Hayworth, Washburn School
Irene Hayzen, Webb Lower School
Laura Heald, Vineyards Elementary School
Jessica Heatherly, Amherst Elementary
Mrs. Hefty, Karns Elementary
Dorrie Hess, Latimer Lane School
Laura Hietpas, Fairglen Elementary School
Teresa Hill, South Knoxville Elementary
Mary Himes, Kingston Elementary
Kathleen Holder, John Harshaw School
Carolyn Hollaway, Vineyards Elementary School
Nancy Holloway, Kingston Elementary
Michelle Horsey, Allison Elementary
Jeff Horwitz, Mary Institute and St. Louis Country Day School
S. Howard, Fairfax Elementary
Kathy Irons, Sharon Hill Elementary School
Pamela James-Powers, Margaret Chase Smith School
Jeana Jarmon, Webb Lower School
Brenda Johnson, Maryville Middle School
Dana Johnson, Fern Bluff Elementary
David Johnson, Robert Sanders School
Julie Johnson, Mary Institute and St. Louis Country Day School
Kim Johnson, Maryville Middle School
Lisa Johnson, Holly Oak School
Joyce A. Joyce, Pennell Elementary School
Louise A. Kanaley, French Road Elementary School
Jennifer Kauffman, Brickey-McCloud Elementary
Guy Kelm, Lincoln School
Jeanne Kemper, Eagleton Elementary
Jane Kershner, Park Lane Elementary School
Sharon Ketts, Archer Community School
Mrs. Khaddouma, Pond Gap
Laura Kildare, Richard Yoakley Alternative School
Angela King, Vineyards Elementary School
Lynn Klempner, Russell School
Judith Kolbenschlag, Harry L. Johnson School
Janet Kornegay, Kingston Elementary
Ethel Kozak, Fairglen Elementary School
Elyse Kushel, Sea Cliff School
Kristin Ladha, Pond Gap
Maureen Lamberti, Sea Cliff School
Terrie Lang, Fairglen Elementary School
Mrs. Larue, Karns Elementary
Sandra Lee, Mary Institute and St. Louis Country Day School
Lynn Leslie, Glenwood Landing
Mattie Lewis, Wallingford Elementary School
Rosina Lizzul, P.S. 130 Brooklyn
Mary Lou Lohr, Walnut Street Elementary School

Mrs. Lorin, Karns Elementary
Lisa Lynch, Northwest Middle
Janet Lyon, The King's Academy
Cathy Cummings Lyttle, Adamsville School
Amelia Mahlstadt, Brentwood Elementary
Lois Makucin, Clover Street School
Rachel J. Malkuch, Trinity Lutheran School
Betty J. Maness, Toby Farms Elementary School
Eleni Mantikas, Sea Cliff School
Terri Maples, Pond Gap
Miriam Marecek, Early Childhood Education,
    Boston University
Marianne Marino, Central School
Amy Marion, Webb Lower School
Sandra Markon, The Rashi School
Renee Martin, Media, PA
Travis Martin, The Learn Center
Judy Matsko, Amoslana School
Angela Matt, Loomis School
Amanda Matthews, Fern Bluff Elementary
Mattson, Kingston Elementary
Christen Mayes, Webb Lower School
Veronica McDermott, Patchogue-Medford Schools
Jane McDevitt, Russell School
Frank McGourty, Miller Elementary
Mollie McKeithan, South Greenville Elementary
Linda McKinley, Fairglen Elementary School
Beth Meyer, Webb Lower School
Kelly Mezza, South Knoxville Elementary
Samantha Miller, South Greenville Elementary
Jeanne Misenheimer, Webb Lower School
Terrie Mitev, Vineyards Elementary School
Moehl, Glenwood Elementary
Jama Mosher, The King's Academy
Mary Ellen Moyher, Springdale School
Ellen M. Mullins, Green Ridge Elementary School
Ellie Murray, Culbertson Elementary School
Helen Naab, Loomis Elementary School
Mrs. Napier, Karns Elementary
Jean Nash, Claude Chester Elementary School
Sherry Nash, Russell School
Kathy Navarre, Pennell Elementary School
Rebecca Nease, Elmhurst Elementary
Joan Neugeborn, Sea Cliff School
Kathleen Nevins, Concord Elementary School
Mrs. Nicely, Karns Elementary
Judy Nord, Mary Institute and St. Louis Country
    Day School
Mimi Olsen, Guggenheim School
Sally Osborn, Morristown East High
Samantha Owens, Ritta Elementary
Cheryl Papa, Hillcrest School
Maryann M. Parker, Whitney Point Middle School
Lori Parton, Washburn School

Linda Pascucci, Sea Cliff School
Amanda Pasternak, Parrottsville Elementary
Joanne Payne-Lionetti, Marion Street School
Jenny Paynter, Fairview Elementary
Dr. Joan Pearlman, The Pingry School
Pat Pendergast, Worrall School
Mrs. Perkins, Karns Elementary
Debbie Peterson, Northwest Middle
Robin Peterson, Green Park Elementary
Tim Peterson, Eagleton Elementary
Marilyn Pickett, Maryville Middle School
Alison Pierce, Morristown East High
Candice Pitney, The King's Academy
Deborah G. Pot, Pennell Elementary School
Mona Potter, Priscilla Purse, Fairglen Elementary School
Becky Pursley, Barton Hills Elementary
Quesinberry, The King's Academy
Tammy Ranger, Skowhegan Area Middle School
Linda Ratta, Claude Chester School
Ray, Pond Gap
Peg Reed, Wickliffe School
Scott Reed, Richard Yoakley Alternative School
Donna Reihing, Glenwood Landing
Marilyn Renfrew, Margaret Chase Smith School
Deborah Revels, Fairglen Elementary School
T. Rhodes, Fairfax Elementary
Rice, Glenwood Elementary
Arlene Roberts, Sea Cliff School
Kristie Roberts, Pond Gap
Mrs. Roberts, Karns Elementary
Robinson, Pond Gap
Sarah Robinson, Northwest Middle
Nancy Rogalsky, Farm Hill School
Linda Rohlfs, Martin School
Tonya Rollins, The King's Academy
Molly Rosenberg, Pennell Elementary School
Nancy Roser, University of Texas
Rosemary Ross, Oak Ridge Alternative School
Anita Rousseau, Richard Yoakley Alternative School
Royster, Fairfax Elementary
D. Rutherford, Oak Ridge Alternative School
Maria Saccardi, Glenwood Landing
Jill Sampson, Webb Lower School
Amanda Sanders, South Knoxville Elementary
Toni Sandlin, Culbertson Elementary School
Maureen Sato, Holly Oak School
Kristi Savage, Washburn School
Mrs. Schneider, Karns Elementary
Millie Seeds, Culbertson Elementary School
Francis Seiler, Webb Lower School
Katherine Shuter, Concord Elementary School
Antonetta Simmone, New Roberto Clemente
Darlene Skaee, Glenwood Landing
Mary Small, Worrall School

# Acknowledgments

Michela Solomita, Glenwood Landing
Susan Soxman, Worrall School
Theresa Sparlin, Pilgrim Lutheran
Dr. Nick Spennato, Media, PA
Vicki Sporsen, St. John Neumann Catholic
Rebecca C. Stanley-Deist, Orchard Farm Elementary
Elena Starr, Concord Elementary
John Steczak, Rose Tree Elementary School
Rhoda J. Steiger, Stillmeadow School
Ann Stevenson, Green Ridge Elementary School
Cynthia Steverson, Webb Lower School
Linda Stickney, Vineyards Elementary School
Adam Stone, Richard Yoakley Alternative School
Cheryl Stroud, Community School District Two
Ed Sullivan, Lake City Middle School
Natalie Sue Svrcek, Brentwood Elementary
Dr. Elizabeth Swaggerty, East Carolina University
Alison Tate, Ritta Elementary
Sherry Tavegie, Meadow Lark Grade School
Ms. Taylor, Karns Elementary
Jennie Teti, Russell School
Laurie Thomas, Guggenheim School
Wanda Thomas, Highland Park School
Jane Tierney, Brentwood Elementary
Jean Tobin, Green Park Elementary
Patricia Towne, Parkside Elementary School
Maureen Tracy, Parkside Elementary School
Barbara Tucker, Springdale School
Phyllis E. Tyler, Walnut Street Elementary School
Julianne Uanino, Sea Cliff School
Elaine Vandiver, Kingston Elementary
Lucy Van Hoff, Glenwood Landing
Susan Wagner, Porter Elementary
Margaret Wales, Pennell Elementary School
Marilyn Walsh, Agassiz School
Dr. Barbara Ward, Washington State University
Marie Wardynski, Delcroft Elementary School

Pam Warren, Lincoln Elementary
Rosa Washington, Fairfax Elementary
Donna Waters, Mary Institute and St. Louis Country
    Day School
Mrs. Watkins, Karns Elementary
Watson, Glenwood Elementary
Kate Watson, Barton Hills Elementary
Chris Weil, Locust Valley Intermediate
Lori Weingust, Sea Cliff School
Renee Weinstein, Loomis Elementary School
Kelli White, Galindo Elementary
Sonia C. Williams, Elmhurst Elementary
Barbara Winslow, Bloomfield Elementary
Paul Wolf Jr., North Middle School
Patricia Wolff, P.S. 41 Manhattan
Janice Wolin, Glenwood Landing
Daphne Wood, Ainsworth Elementary
Patricia Woody, John Harshaw School
Deborah Wooten, P.S. 126 Manhattan
Mrs. A. Wright, Karns Elementary
Mrs. L. Wright, Karns Elementary
Pat Wright, Webb Lower School
Anne Wuthrich, Vineyards Elementary School
Lauren Wyatt, Ensworth High School
Kerry Yandrasits, Sea Cliff School
Joanne Zeccarelli, Vineyards Elementary School
Victoria Zell, South Greenville Elementary


And thanks also to Valerie Hess, Hofstra University;
Ann Lovett, Manhasset, New York; and Katie Wooten,
Knoxville, Tennessee, for tabulating children's responses.

The title for this book was taken from Lilian Moore's
poem "If You Catch a Firefly."

# Contents

# Contents

Dedicated to Jonathan Paul Cullinan (1969–1975),
a boy who loved poetry

This award stemmed from Jonathan's tragic death.
The boy depicted in the emblem of the NCTE Award
for Poetry for Children is in his honor.
—*B.C.* and *D.W.*

*The National Council of Teachers of English*
*Award for Excellence in Poetry for Children*
*is presented once every three years to a poet*
*for a distinguished body of work sustained over a period of time*
*and honors the memory of Jonathan Paul Cullinan,*
*a child who loved books.*

# Introduction

All fifteen poets featured in this book have received an important award: the National Council of Teachers of English Award for Excellence in Poetry for Children. The award, given to poets judged to be the *very best*, is for the entire body of their work, rather than a single book or poem. From 1977 to 1982, the award was bestowed once each year. Since then, it has been given every three years. This book celebrates these accomplished award winners.

How were the poems selected? The process was similar to the one used to create the original book, *A Jar of Tiny Stars*. Teachers and librarians across the United States asked their students to vote for their favorite poems from a sampling written by each author. More than four thousand students listened to and read the poems, then ranked their top five choices for each poet. The poems receiving the most votes from the students appear in this book. This national field test showed that students prefer poetry that makes them laugh, that has rhyme and rhythm, and that connects with their lives.

Bernice E. Cullinan
Professor Emeritus, New York University
Editor in Chief, Wordsong

Deborah Wooten
Associate Professor, University of Tennessee

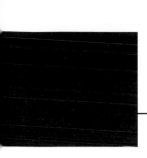

*"One of my teachers told me, 'Never let a day go by without looking on three beautiful things.' I try to live up to that and find it isn't difficult. The sky in all weathers is, for me, the first of these three things."*

—David McCord

# Every Time I Climb a Tree

Every time I climb a tree
Every time I climb a tree
Every time I climb a tree
I scrape a leg
Or skin a knee
And every time I climb a tree
I find some ants
Or dodge a bee
And get the ants
All over me

And every time I climb a tree
Where have you been?
They say to me
But don't they know that I am free
Every time I climb a tree?
I like it best
To spot a nest
That has an egg
or maybe three

And then I skin
The other leg
But every time I climb a tree
I see a lot of things to see
Swallows rooftops and TV
And all the fields and farms there be
Every time I climb a tree
Though climbing may be good for ants
It isn't awfully good for pants
But still it's pretty good for me
Every time I climb a tree

# THE PICKETY FENCE

The pickety fence
The pickety fence
Give it a lick it's
The pickety fence
Give it a lick it's
A clickety fence
Give it a lick it's
A lickety fence
Give it a lick
Give it a lick
Give it a lick
With a rickety stick
Pickety
Pickety
Pickety
Pick

# Snowman

My little snowman has a mouth,
So he is always smiling south.
My little snowman has a nose;
I couldn't seem to give him toes,
I couldn't seem to make his ears.
He shed a lot of frozen tears
Before I gave him any eyes—
But they are big ones for his size.

# THE STAR IN THE PAIL

I took the pail for water when the sun was high
And left it in the shadow of the barn nearby.

When evening slippered over like the moth's brown wing,
I went to fetch the water from the cool wellspring.

The night was clear and warm and wide, and I alone
Was walking by the light of stars as thickly sown

As wheat across the prairie, or the first fall flakes,
Or spray upon the lawn—the kind the sprinkler makes.

But every star was far away as far can be,
With all the starry silence sliding over me.

And every time I stopped I set the pail down slow,
For when I stooped to pick the handle up to go

Of all the stars in heaven there was one to spare,
And he silvered in the water and I left him there.

# I Have a Book

that has no cover
where there used to be a lady
and her knighted lover.
Oh, her lover was a knight
and his armor fitted right.
While he hadn't any horse,
still I always thought he might;
and I always thought of course
he'd be riding far away,
for the day was good and bright
though the tree was big and shady.
Now there isn't any lady
and there isn't any knight,
and there never was a horse,
so there never was a fight.
And the book all by itself
is sort of lonely on the shelf.

*"The highlight of each day is a walk with my dog and a friend and her dog on one of the many trails nearby. This keeps me in touch with the weather, the wildlife, and the wonderful scenery in every direction."*

—Aileen Fisher

# My Puppy

I have a playful
prankish pup:

When I stoop down
he prances up

And snuffs my neck
and slicks my ear

As if I'd been
away a *year*.

I say, "Be good,
you prankish pup."

But he just smiles
and eats me up!

# MY CAT AND I

When I flop down
to take a rest
my cat jumps up
upon my chest.

She kneads my sweater
with her paws . . .
and sometimes even
uses claws.

She rubs my chin
and purrs away,
as if I am
a game to play!

# Cricket Jackets

The day a cricket's jacket
gets pinchy, he can crack it
and hang it on a bracket
as he goes hopping by.

He doesn't need a mother
to go and buy another,
he doesn't need a mother,
and I will tell you why:

Beneath the pinchy jacket
the cricket sheds with vigor
he has a new one growing
that's just a little bigger,
to last him till July.

And then, again, he'll crack it,
his pinchy cricket jacket,
and hang it on a bracket
as he goes hopping by.

# Out in the Dark and Daylight

Out in the dark and daylight,
under a cloud or tree,

Out in the park and play light,
out where the wind blows free,

Out in the March or May light
with shadows and stars to see,

Out in the dark and daylight . . .
that's where I like to be.

# Listen, Rabbit!

I saw him first
when the sun went down
in the summer sky
at the edge of town
where grass grew green
and the path grew brown.

I couldn't tell
what he was at all
when I saw him first,
sort of halfway small,
sort of halfway grown,
near a gray old stone
in the field, alone.

Then I saw his ears
standing rabbit tall!

I stood as still
as a maple tree
and I looked at him
and he looked at me . . .
with only one eye
that I could see,
bulging out
on the side of his head.

"Nice little rabbit,"
I softly said
inside myself,
though I hoped he'd hear
with two long ears
standing up so near
and my thoughts so clear.

My heart went thump!
And do you know why?
'Cause I hoped that maybe
as time went by
the rabbit and I
(if he felt like *me*)
could have each other
for company.

Note: This is only part of "Listen, Rabbit!" Read the entire poem in Aileen Fisher's book
*Listen, Rabbit!*

"*If there were a recipe for a poem, these would be the ingredients: word sounds, rhythm, description, feeling, memory, rhyme, and imagination. They can be put together a thousand different ways, a thousand, thousand . . . more.*"

—Karla Kuskin

# Hughbert and the Glue

Hughbert had a jar of glue.
From Hugh the glue could not be parted,
At least could not be parted far,
For Hugh was glued to Hughbert's jar.
But that is where it all had started.
The glue upon the shoe of Hugh
Attached him to the floor.
The glue on Hughbert's gluey hand
Was fastened to the door,
While two of Hughbert's relatives
Were glued against each other.
His mother, I believe, was one.
The other was his brother.
The dog and cat stood quite nearby.
They could not move from there.
The bird was glued securely
Into Hughbert's mother's hair.

Hughbert's father hurried home
And loudly said to Hugh:
"From now on I would rather
That you did not play with glue."

# The Meal

Timothy Tompkins had turnips and tea.
The turnips were tiny.
He ate at least three.
And then, for dessert,
He had onions and ice.
He liked that so much
That he ordered it twice.
He had two cups of ketchup,
A prune, and a pickle.
"Delicious," said Timothy.
"Well worth a nickel."
He folded his napkin
And hastened to add,
"It's one of the loveliest breakfasts I've had."

# I Woke Up This Morning

I woke up this morning
At quarter past seven.
I kicked up the covers
And stuck out my toe.

And ever since then
(That's a quarter past seven)
They haven't said anything
Other than "no."

They haven't said anything
Other than "Please, dear,
Don't do what you're doing,"
Or "Lower your voice."

Whatever I've done
And however I've chosen,
I've done the wrong thing
And I've made the wrong choice.

I didn't wash well
And I didn't say thank you.
I didn't shake hands
And I didn't say please.

I didn't say sorry
When passing the candy
I banged the box into
Miss Witelson's knees.
I didn't say sorry.
I didn't stand straighter.
I didn't speak louder
When asked what I'd said.

Well, I said
That tomorrow
At quarter past seven
They can
Come in and get me.
I'm Staying in Bed.

# WINTER CLOTHES

Under my hood I have a hat
And under that
My hair is flat.
Under my coat
My sweater's blue.
My sweater's red.
I'm wearing two.
My muffler muffles to my chin
And round my neck
And then tucks in.
My gloves were knitted
By my aunts.
I've mittens too
And pants
And pants
And boots
And shoes
With socks inside.
The boots are rubber, red and wide.
And when I walk
I must not fall
Because I can't get up at all.

# Lewis Has a Trumpet

A trumpet
A trumpet
Lewis has a trumpet
A bright one that's yellow
A loud proud horn.
He blows it in the evening
When the moon is newly rising
He blows it when it's raining
In the cold and misty morn
It honks and it whistles
It roars like a lion
It rumbles like a lion
With a wheezy huffing hum
His parents say it's awful
Oh really simply awful
But
Lewis says he loves it
It's such a handsome trumpet
And when he's through with trumpets
He's going to buy a drum.

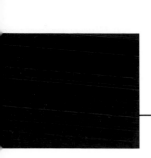

"When I watched my young daughter trying to learn how to roller-skate, I wrote '74th Street.' 'Hey, this little kid gets roller skates. / She puts them on. / She stands up and almost / flops over backwards. . . .'

"My daughter starting, then falling, then starting again with many kinds of movements inspired a different sort of poem. . . . The words, the sound of them, needed to fit the content of what they said."

—Myra Cohn Livingston

# Kittens

Our cat had kittens
weeks ago
when everything outside was snow.

So she stayed in
and kept them warm
and safe from all the clouds and storm.

But yesterday
when there was sun
she snuzzled on the smallest one

and turned it over
from beneath
and took its fur between her teeth

and carried it
outside to see
how nice a winter day can be

and then our dog
decided he
would help her take the other three

and one by one
they took them out
to see what sun is all about

so when they're grown
they'll always know
to never be afraid of snow.

# Lemonade Stand

Every summer
under the shade
we fix up a stand
to sell lemonade.

A stack of cups,
a pitcher of ice,
a shirtboard sign
to tell the price.

A dime for the big,
A nickel for small.
The nickel cup's short.
The dime cup's tall.

Plenty of sugar
to make it sweet,
and sometimes cookies
for us to eat.

But when the sun
moves into the shade
it gets too hot
to sell lemonade.

Nobody stops
so we put things away
and drink what's left
and start to play.

# Arthur Thinks on Kennedy

When Kennedy
Come to our town
He come with dreams
Got shot right down.

It rained all morning.
You can bet
They didn't want him
Getting wet.

They put a bubble
On his car
So we could see him
From afar.

But then the sun
Come out, so they
Just took the bubble
Clean away.

When Kennedy
Come to our town
Some low-down white folks
Shot him down,

And I got bubbles,
I got dreams,
So I know what
That killing means.

# Shell

When it was time
for Show and Tell,
Adam brought a big pink shell.

He told about
the ocean roar
and walking on the sandy shore.

And then he passed
the shell around.
We listened to the water sound.

And that's the first time
I could hear
the wild waves calling to my ear.

# Martin Luther King

Got me a special place
For Martin Luther King.
His picture on the wall
Makes me sing.

I look at it for a long time
And think of some
Real good ways
We will overcome.

# Eve Merriam

*"I've sometimes spent weeks looking for precisely the right word. It's like having a tiny marble in your pocket, you can just feel it. Sometimes you find a word and say, 'No, I don't think this is it. . . .' Then you discard it, and take another and another until you get it right. I do think poetry is great fun. That's what I'd like to stress more than anything else: the joy of the sounds of language."*

—Eve Merriam

Gooseberry,
Juice berry,
Loose berry jam.

Gooseberry,
Juice berry,
Loose berry jam.

Gooseberry,
Juice berry,
Loose berry jam.

Spread it on crackers,
Spread it on bread,
Try not to spread it
Onto your head.

No matter how neatly
You try to bite in,
It runs like a river
Down to your chin.

# How to Eat a Poem

Don't be polite.
Bite in.
Pick it up with your fingers and lick the juice that
        may run down your chin.
It is ready and ripe now, whenever you are.

You do not need a knife or fork or spoon
        or plate or napkin or tablecloth.

For there is no core
or stem
or rind
or pit
or seed
or skin
to throw away.

# Skip Rope Rhyme for Our Time

Junk mail, junk mail,
look look look:
bargain offer coupon,
catalogue book.

Junk mail, junk mail,
free free free:
trial sample,
guarantee.

Here's an offer
you can't let pass:
an artificial lawn
with real crab grass.

Twenty cents off,
just go to the store
and buy what you don't want,
then buy some more.

Junk mail, junk mail,
what's my name?
My name is Dear Occupant
and yours is the same.

# Windshield Wiper

| | |
|---|---|
| fog smog | fog smog |
| tissue paper | tissue paper |
| clear the blear | clear the smear |
| | |
| fog more | fog more |
| splat splat | downpour |
| | |
| rubber scraper | rubber scraper |
| overshoes | macintosh |
| bumbershoot | muddle on |
| slosh through | slosh through |
| | |
| drying up | drying up |
| sky lighter | sky lighter |
| nearly clear | nearly clear |

clearing clearing veer

clear here clear

# Umbilical

You can take away my mother,
you can take away my sister,
but don't take away
my little transistor.

I can do without sunshine,
I can do without Spring,
but I can't do without
my ear to that thing.

I can live without water,
in a hole in the ground,
but I can't live without
that sound that sound that sound that sOWnd.

# John Ciardi

*"Poetry and learning are both fun, and children are full of an enormous relish for both. My poetry is just a bubbling up of a natural foolishness, and the idea that maybe you can make language dance a bit."*

—John Ciardi

# MUMMY SLEPT LATE AND DADDY FIXED BREAKFAST

Daddy fixed the breakfast.
He made us each a waffle.
It looked like gravel pudding.
It tasted something awful.

"Ha, ha," he said, "I'll try again.
This time I'll get it right."
But what *I* got was in between
Bituminous and anthracite.

"A little too well done? Oh well,
I'll have to start all over."
*That* time what landed on my plate
Looked like a manhole cover.

I tried to cut it with a fork:
The fork gave off a spark.
I tried a knife and twisted it
Into a question mark.

I tried it with a hack-saw.
I tried it with a torch.
It didn't even make a dent.
It didn't even scorch.

The next time Dad gets breakfast
When Mummy's sleeping late,
I think I'll skip the waffles.
I'd sooner eat the plate!

# What Did You Learn at the Zoo?

What did I learn at the zoo?
Monkeys look like you.

Some are bald and some have curls,
But monkeys look like boys and girls.

Some are quiet and some make noise,
But all of them look like girls and boys.

What did *you* learn at the zoo?
Oh, much the same as you:

Gorillas are good, gorillas are bad,
But all of them look a lot like Dad.

Some do one thing, some another,
But all of them scream a lot like Mother.

What did *we* learn at the zoo?
Just what we wanted to:

That it's fun to tease if you make it rhyme
(Though you mustn't do it all the time),
That kangaroos hop and monkeys climb,
*And* that a bottle of lemon-and-lime
Is a very good way to spend a dime.

(And so is a bag of peanuts.)

# The Happy Family

Before the children say goodnight,
        Mother, Father, stop and think:
Have you screwed their heads on tight?
        Have you washed their ears with ink?

Have you said and done and thought
        All that earnest parents should?
Have you beat them as you ought?
        Have you begged them to be good?

And above all—when you start
        Out the door and douse the light—
Think, be certain, search your heart:
        Have you screwed their heads on tight?

If they sneeze when they're asleep,
        Will their little heads come off?
If they just breathe very deep?
        If—especially—they cough?

Should—alas!—the little dears
        Lose a little head or two,
Have you inked their little ears:
        Girls' ears pink and boys' ears blue?

Children's heads are very loose.
        Mother, Father, screw them tight.
If you feel uncertain use
        A monkey wrench, but do it right.

If a head should come unscrewed
        You will know that you have failed.
Doubtful cases should be glued.
        Stubborn cases should be nailed.

Then when all your darlings go
        Sweetly screaming off to bed,
Mother, Father, you may know
        Angels guard each little head.

Come the morning you will find
        One by one each little head
Full of gentle thoughts and kind,
        Sweetly screaming to be fed.

# *Sometimes* I Feel This Way

I have one head that wants to be good,
        And one that wants to be bad.
And always, as soon as I get up,
        One of my heads is sad.

"Be bad," says one head. "Don't you know
        It's fun to be bad. Be as bad as you like.
Put sand in your brother's shoe—that's fun.
        Put gum on the seat of your sister's bike."

"What fun is that?" says my other head.
        "Why not go down before the rest
And set things out for breakfast? My,
        That would please Mother. Be good—that's best."

"What! Better than putting frogs in the sink?
        Or salt in the tea-pot? Have some fun.
Be bad, be bad, be good and bad.
        You know it is good to be bad," says One.

"Is it good to make Sister and Brother sad?
        And Mother and Daddy? And when you do,
Is it good to get spanked? Is it good to cry?
        No, no. Be good—that's best," says Two.

So one by one they say what they say,
      And what they say is "Be Good—Be Bad."
And if One is happy that makes Two cry.
      And if Two is happy that makes One sad.

Someday maybe, when I grow up,
      I shall wake and find I have just one—
The happy head. But which will it be?
      I wish I knew. They are both *some* fun.

# Summer Song

By the sand between my toes,
By the waves behind my ears,
By the sunburn on my nose,
By the little salty tears
That make rainbows in the sun
When I squeeze my eyes and run,
By the way the seagulls screech,
Guess where I am? *At the . . . !*
By the way the children shout
Guess what happened? *School is . . . !*
By the way I sing this song
Guess if summer lasts too long:
You must answer Right or . . . !

*"Poetry should be like fireworks, packed carefully and artfully, ready to explode with unpredictable effects. When people asked Robert Frost—as they did by the hundreds—what he meant by 'But I have promises to keep / And miles to go before I sleep / And miles to go before I sleep,' he always turned the question aside with a joke. Maybe he couldn't answer it, and maybe he was glad that the lines exploded in so many different colors in so many people's minds."*

—Lilian Moore

# If You Catch a Firefly

If you catch a firefly
        and keep it in a jar
You may find that
        you have lost
A tiny star.

It you let it go then,
        back into the night,
You may see it
        once again
Star bright.

# I Left My Head

I left my head
somewhere
today.
Put it down for
just
a minute.
Under the
table?
On a chair?
Wish I were
able
to say
where.
Everything I need
is
in it!

# Mine

I made a sand castle.
In rolled the sea.
      "All sand castles
      belong to me—
      to me,"
said the sea.

I dug sand tunnels.
In flowed the sea.
      "All sand tunnels
      belong to me—
      to me,"
said the sea.

I saw my sand pail floating free.
I ran and snatched it from the sea.
      "My sand pail
      belongs to me—
      to ME!"

# Recess

The children
scribble their shadows
on the school yard,

scribble
scribble
on a great blackboard—

lanky leg
shadows
running into
lifted arm shadows
flinging
bouncing ball shapes
into skinny upside down shadows
swinging
on
long monkey bars

till
a cloud
moving
across the morning sun
wipes out all
scribbles
like a giant
eraser.

# Construction

The giant mouth
chews
rocks
spews them
and is back for
more.

The giant arm
swings up
with a girder
for
the fourteenth floor,

Down there,
a tiny man
is
telling them
where
to put a skyscraper.

"*Most of the time, almost all of the time, I want my poems to do more than prose can do. So if I want to just say, 'Dear Mom, I am fine at camp,' I don't have to write a poem. But if I'm going to be a poet, if I'm poeting, if I'm writing poems, I want to do more in my poems than just present facts or feelings or communicate. I want my poems to sing as well as to say.*"

—Arnold Adoff

# Flavors

Mama is chocolate:  you must be swirls
                              of dark fudge,
                    and ripples
                                        through
                    your cocoa
                              curls;
chips
            and
flips of sprinkles
            on your
                    summer
                    face.

# Flavors

Daddy is vanilla:  you must be mean
                                                old
                                    bean
                    in the morning,
                    cherry
                    chunks by afternoon,
                    and
                              sweet
                              peach sometimes.

But mostly     you
               are vanilla
                              up
               your
               arms.

# Flavors

Me
is better
   butter:    I must be
           pecans
               roasted,
               toasted;

almond
wal nut   three
        scoop combination
            cone:
melting under
     kisses.

It is a new color.
It is a new flavor.
    For
      love.

Coach Says: Listen Sonny, You Are The Safety On This Team,
And Your Body Belongs To Me, And Your Safety Is The Last
Thing On Your Mind. Right? Right. Their Guy Is Super Fast.
Do Not Let Him Get Past. Period. Understood? Safety Last.
Now Play It By The Numbers.


Simple.
     We start with eleven    when the whistle blows,
     and
          their quarterback    throws his pass.
                                      Simple.

Number One:    He throws the ball.
Number Two:    The ball is caught.
Number Three:  Their receiver runs
                d o w n   the field
                       toward me.
Number Four
Through Ten:    My team
           mates  who ought to stop him  are hit
       or
       fall,  or  miss,  or  are  too  slow  to  make
                               the play.

Simple.
     Safety last. I  am  the  last  of  our  eleven,
           and the runner    runs my way.

# black is brown is tan

black    is brown    is tan
is girl    is boy
is nose    is face
is all the colors
of the race

is dark    is light
singing songs
in singing night
kiss big woman    hug big man
black    is brown    is tan
this is the way it is for us    this is the way we are

Note: This is only part of "black is brown is tan." Read the entire poem in Arnold Adoff's book *black is brown is tan*.

# Valerie Worth

"*Never forget that the subject is as important as your feeling: The mud puddle itself is as important as your pleasure in looking at it or splashing through it. Never let the mud puddle get lost in the poetry—because, in many ways, the mud puddle* is *the poetry.*"

—Valerie Worth

# dinosaurs

Dinosaurs
Do not count,
Because
They are all
Dead:

None of us
Saw them, dogs
Do not even
Know that
They were there—

But they
Still walk
About heavily
In everybody's
Head.

# lawnmower

The lawnmower
Grinds its teeth
Over the grass,
Spitting out a thick
Green spray;

Its head is too full
Of iron and oil
To know
What it throws
Away:

The lawn's whole
Crop of chopped
Soft,
Delicious
Green hay.

# giraffe

How lucky
To live
So high
Above
The body,
Breathing
At heaven's
Level,
Looking
Sun
In the eye;
While down
Below
The neck's
Precarious
Stair,
Back, belly,
And legs
Take care
Of themselves,
Hardly
Aware
Of the head's
Airy
Affairs.

# safety pin

Closed, it sleeps
On its side
Quietly,
The silver
Image
Of some
Small fish;

Opened, it snaps
Its tail out
Like a thin
Shrimp, and looks
At the sharp
Point with a
Surprised eye.

# pebbles

Pebbles belong to no one
Until you pick them up—
Then they are yours.

But which, of all the world's
Mountains of little broken stones,
Will you choose to keep?

The smooth black, the white,
The rough gray with sparks
Shining in its cracks?

Somewhere the best pebble must
Lie hidden, meant for you
If you can find it.

*"I think about the images first and the rhyme only incidentally. With rhyme you always have a sense of what's coming at the end of the line, and that ruins the surprise. To me, poetry should knock your block off."*

—Barbara Juster Esbensen

# Bat

Every night
a short word
covered with fur   mouth open
flies
out of dark libraries

All day it hangs
upside-down in the card
catalog    under B

But at sundown    BAT
by the hundreds
leaves the gloomy
pages
of mystery books    crawls
out of damp bindings
and    glides   into the night air
shaking itself free
of the trailing old words
DRACULA   BLOOD   FANG. . .

# Elephant

The word is too heavy
to lift    too cumbersome to
lead through a room filled with
relatives or small
glass trinkets

ELEPHANT

He must have invented it
himself. This is a lumbering
gray word    the ears of it
are huge and flap like loose
wings    a word with
wrinkled knees and toes
like boxing gloves

This word    ELEPHANT
sways toward us    bulk
and skull-bones filling up
the space    trumpeting
its own wide name
through its nose!

# MY CAT

My cat is asleep—white paws
folded under
his chin     He is a soft gray
smudge on the round rug

Dozing in the sun
He is a warm round stone
with a fur collar

My cat is taking
a nap     Not a whisker
trembles     Not a hair
moves     His breath goes
softly in and out

Stay in your holes
mice!     My cat sees you
in his dreams
and he has left
his motor running!

# SNAKE

The word begins to
hiss as soon as the first
letter
goes on     S
s-s-s-s-s-s-s     forked tongue flickers
Hard eyes stare

Already the rest of the poem
shrinks back from
his narrow speed     The paper
draws in its breath     SNAKE
loops around the pencil
slides
among typewriter keys     slips
like a silk shoelace
away

# PENCILS

The rooms in a pencil
are narrow
but elephants     castles and
watermelons
fit in

In a pencil
noisy words yell for attention
and quiet words wait their turn

How did they slip
into such a tight place?
Who
gives them their
lunch?

From a broken pencil
an unbroken poem will come!
There is a long story living
in the shortest pencil

Every word in your
pencil
is fearless    ready to walk
the blue tightrope lines
Ready
to teeter and smile
down    Ready to come right out
and show you
thinking!

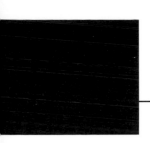

"*I love to write poetry for the same reason that I love to read it. It's music. I can hear it and feel it. Writing poetry allows me to make my own music by combining syllables and silences, rhythm and melody. I go to that place in my head where thoughts and images take shape and new people are born. It's a magical place, and I am very grateful that it exists.*"

—Eloise Greenfield

# Lucky Little Birds

They're lucky little birds
they don't have to hear
their parents over and over again
say, "Chew your food, now, dear."

They never have to try
to turn their food into pulp
they only have to open their mouths
and gulp

# Rope Rhyme

Get set, ready now, jump right in
Bounce and kick and giggle and spin
Listen to the rope when it hits the ground
Listen to that clappedy-slappedy sound
Jump right up when it tells you to
Come back down, whatever you do
Count to a hundred, count by ten
Start to count all over again
That's what jumping is all about
Get set, ready now,
                    jump
                      right
                        out!

# The Sailboat Race

The boats are ready
to race
each wants to sail
at the fastest pace
they're ready to ride
the water's wings
and listen as the wind sings
a tale of those who have
sailed before
the boats are ready
to soar
to turn their sails
against the air
that pushes them
from here to there
they hear the signal
to start the chase
to see who will win
in the sailboat race
*and they're off!*

# To Friendship

It's time for the party
and as we begin
let's do a sentimental
thing
let's lift our punch
to the bunch
(that's us)
we'll say that our
friendship is dear and
we'll promise to keep it from
year to year
and
this toast we'll repeat
each time we meet
and now, my friends—
let's eat

# THOUGHTS

I stand in the center
and make the traffic flow
for people whose names
I don't even know

Who are these people
I never meet
where are they going
and what do they do
when they're not riding
down my street?

"To tell the truth, I often start writing without an idea in my head. A line of words will pop into mind and then I'll look for something to rhyme with it. That makes two lines. Then I see what else I can say, and go on rhyming. Once in a while, though, an idea will lead to a poem. It sometimes comes when I ask myself a crazy question, like, what if dinosaurs were alive today? Or, what if a bowl of gravy were full of exploding torpedoes?"

—X. J. Kennedy

# THE UNICORN I TRIED TO PAINT

The unicorn I tried to paint
Has ended up a cow.
My teacher looked and said, "How quaint."
There's trouble on her brow—

My cow's, I mean. She looks as though
Her horn had slightly slipped.
She has worse problems down below.
My paintbrush must have dripped.

Was such a creature ever born?
I'll keep her anyhow.
She's realer than a unicorn,
My cockeyed unicow.

# Pacifier

Nights when Robert starts to blubber
Mother plugs his mouth with rubber,

A squirmy little chewy knob
He bites on and forgets to sob.

Once I picked one up and bit.
What do babies see in it?

# Basketball Bragging

Agatha Goop with a whale of a whoop
Swept a swisher through the hoop.

She told her teammates, "There you are!
You guys are dog meat! I'm the star!"

Her teammates knew just what to do:
They dribbled her down and dunked her through.

Now Agatha's nose may be out of joint,
But she had to admit that they'd made their point.

# Mixed-Up School

We have a crazy mixed-up school.
Our teacher Mrs. Cheetah
Makes us talk backwards. Nicer cat
You wouldn't want to meet a.

To start the day we eat our lunch,
Then do some heavy dome-work.
The boys' and girls' rooms go to us,
The hamster marks our homework.

At recess time we race inside
To put on diving goggles,
Play pin-the-donkey-on-the-tail,
Ball-foot or ap-for-bobbles.

Old Cheetah, with a chunk of chalk,
Writes right across two blackbirds,
And when she says, "Go home!" we walk
The whole way barefoot backwards.

# Martin Luther King Day

Solemn bells in steeples sing:

*Doctor*
*Martin*
*Luther*
*King.*

He lived his life
He dreamed his dream:
The worst-off people
To redeem,

He dreamed a world
Where people stood
Not separate, but
In brotherhood.

Now ten-ton bells together swing:

*Remember*
*Martin*
*Luther*
*King.*

*"I think that my poems begin in my feet! Nothing gets me started on a poem like a walk. In some uncanny way the steady rhythm of my steps allows new ideas to surface and take hold in my mind. Sometimes the beat comes with words attached; sometimes it is only a wordless cadence that must find its language. But once it manifests itself, I know that sooner or later the poem will follow. This magical confluence of sound and rhythm is always the seed of the poem."*

—Mary Ann Hoberman

# Big Sister

I have a big sister;
She's taller and older;
On tiptoe I only
Reach up to her shoulder;
But I have a secret
That I haven't told her.
    (It's how to grow faster
    Until I grow past her.)

    *I watch what she's eating;*
    *I watch what she's drinking;*
    *I don't let her notice*
    *Or see what I'm thinking;*
    *But each time that she*
    *Takes a bite, I take two;*
    *And that way she only*
    *Eats half what I do.*

I have a big sister;
She's taller and older;
On tiptoe I only
Reach up to her shoulder;
But I have a secret
That I haven't told her.
    (The way I will beat her
    Is just to outeat her!)

# FISH

Look at them flit
Lickety-split
Wiggling
Swiggling
Swerving
Curving
Hurrying
Scurrying
Chasing
Racing
Whizzing
Whisking
Flying
Frisking
Tearing around
With a leap and a bound
But none of them making the tiniest

       tiniest

        tiniest

         tiniest

          sound.

# "Eat It—
# It's Good for You!"

"Eat it—it's good for you!"
    That makes me mad.
How can something good for you
    Taste so bad?

"Try it. You'll like it."
    I know that's a lie.
I know I won't like it
    So why should I try?

"Just take a nibble.
    Just one little taste."
What good is a nibble?
    The rest goes to waste.

Eggplant is icky.
    Spaghetti is fine.
Why can't they eat their food
    And let me eat mine?

# Pick Up Your Room

Pick up your room, my mother says
    (She says it every day);
My room's too heavy to pick up
    (That's what I always say).

Drink up your milk, she says to me,
    Don't bubble like a clown;
Of course she knows I'll answer that
    I'd rather drink it down.

And when she says at eight o'clock,
    You must go right to bed,
We both repeat my answer:
    *Why not go left instead?*

# Our Family Comes from 'Round the World

Our family comes
From 'round the world:
Our hair is straight,
Our hair is curled,
Our eyes are brown,
Our eyes are blue,
Our skins are different
Colors, too.

*Tra la tra la*
*Tra la tra lee*
*We're one big happy family!*

We're girls and boys,
We're big and small,
We're young and old,
We're short and tall.
We're everything
That we can be
And still we are
A family.

*O la dee da*
*O la dee dee*
*We're one big happy family!*

We laugh and cry,
We work and play,
We help each other
Every day.
The world's a lovely
Place to be
Because we are
A family.

*Hurray hurrah*
*Hurrah hurree*
*We're one big happy family!*

"I've always believed that poetry—all writing, really—should be accessible. Writing is a form of communication, after all. So why be obtuse? I didn't realize it when I was young, but this particular mind-set made me a perfect candidate for writing children's poetry."

—Nikki Grimes

# HOT

HOT is a thirsty word that
wakes me from a deep sleep.
I leave my dreams and stumble to the kitchen.
I place the word in the sink, then
turn the cold water on full-blast.

Hot days send me to
the water fountain where my
face goes for a swim.

# WORDS

Sugar
Honey
Sweetie Pie
Shortcake
Cupcake
Sweet Dumplin'
Chocolate Drop—
Seems to me
That love
Might lead
To cavities.

# The Secret

Danitra's scared of pigeons. I promised not to tell,
then I opened my big mouth and out the secret fell.
I tried to shove it right back in, though it was much too late.
I told her I was sorry, but Danitra didn't wait.
"What kind of friend are you?" she yelled before she stomped away.
She wouldn't hardly say a word to me the whole next day.
She finally forgave me, but not until I swore
to never, ever give away a secret anymore.

# Sick Day

I lay down sick this afternoon.
Gorilla knew and came.
She hopped up on the bed with me,
meowing out my name.

She felt my forehead with her paw.
She listened to my heart.
My every cough and toss and turn
gave her a little start.

Cecilia stopped by to make sure
I wasn't getting worse,
and found me curled up peacefully
beside my feline nurse.

# Snow

The word begins to melt
inside my pocket. SNOW.
I fling its lacy coldness
in the air, then watch it
floating there.

Magic! Evening snow
drifts turn each streetlight into
a star on a stick.

# Lee Bennett Hopkins

"*Poetry! There is no other genre like it in the world. A good poem can take you places you never thought possible, wake you up, shake you, make your every emotion quake with excitement and awe. Writing poetry is taking a subject—be it a pigeon or a Popsicle—breathing new life into it, letting readers know they never experienced a moment such as this before.*"

—Lee Bennett Hopkins

# JUST

when
everything
seems
to go
along
just
fine

Life
comes by
and
throws
you
its
line.

# Good Books, Good Times!

Good books.
Good times.
Good stories.
Good rhymes.
Good beginnings.
Good ends.
Good people.
Good friends.
Good fiction.
Good facts.
Good adventures.
Good acts.
Good stories.
Good rhymes.
*Good* books.
*Good* times.

# This Tooth

I jiggled it
    jaggled it
    jerked it.

I pushed
    and pulled
    and poked it.

But—

As soon as I stopped,
and left it alone,
This tooth came out
on its very own!

# CAT'S KIT

Needle-claws
Thimbled paws

Soft,
        silky,
                pincushiony toes—

A
Siamese
seamstress

wherever

she
goes.

# Puppy

We bought our puppy
　　A brand new bed
But he likes sleeping
　　On mine instead.

I'm glad he does
　　'Cause I'd miss his cold nose

Waking me up,
　　Tickling my toes.

About the Poets

# David McCord

"**I** seemed to know instinctively that to write for the young I had to write for myself. I write out of myself, about things I did as a boy, about things that are fairly timeless as subjects. . . .

"Children love words, rhythm, rhyme, music, games. They climb trees, skate, swim, swing, fish, explore, act, ride, run, and love snow and getting wet all over; they make things and are curious about science. They love humor and nonsense and imaginary conversations with imaginary things; they are closer to the sixth sense than we who are older." [1]

## You May Want to Know

David McCord worked at Harvard University for thirty-seven years, serving as fund-raiser, alumni editor, and historian but, all the while, he continued to write poetry for children. He was the author or editor of fifty books of poetry, essays, history, medicine, light verse, and verse for children. He was also an artist and had several one-man shows of watercolor landscapes.

David McCord was awarded the first honorary degree of doctor of humane letters ever granted at Harvard; it was conferred on him at the same ceremonies at which President John F. Kennedy received an LL.D.

In 1983, Simmons College in Boston, Massachusetts, presented him with a doctor of children's literature degree. The citation states:

". . . as a poet who has dedicated your life to the creation of poetry which opens the ears of children to the nuances of language and to the splendors of the world which language represents, you have spoken in a unique voice. You have brought to bear upon your work your long and thorough investigation of and fascination with the natural world, the social world, the world of the intellect, and the world of the imagination.

". . . You have helped awaken adults to the sounds of the child's world. . . . The poet John Ciardi has said, 'One is too few of [you] and there is, alas, no second.'" In 1977 he was the first recipient of the NCTE Award for Excellence in Poetry for Children.

David McCord was born on November 15, 1897, near Greenwich Village, New York City. He grew up on Long Island, in Princeton, New Jersey, and on a ranch by the Rogue River in Oregon. He died in 1997.

"I try to be at my desk four hours a day, from eight a.m. to noon. Ideas come to me out of experiences and from reading and remembering. I usually do a first draft by hand. I can't imagine writing verse on a typewriter, and for years I wrote nothing but verse so I formed the habit of thinking with a pencil or pen in hand. I usually rework my material, sometimes more, sometimes less. I never try out my ideas on children, except on the child I used to know—me! Fortunately, I remember pretty well what I used to like to read, think about, and do. . . . I guess what it amounts to is I never grew up." [2]

## You May Want to Know

Aileen Fisher liked to work with wood she found in the forest; she didn't change its shape but looked for shapes that were already in the wood. Then she polished the wood to bring out its own tendencies. This is similar to the way she worked with words when she wrote poetry; she searched for just the right word and then polished it to bring out the spirit of the poem. [3]

Aileen Fisher was born on September 9, 1906, in Iron River, Michigan. She attended the University of Chicago and received her bachelor of journalism from the University of Missouri. She worked at the Women's Journalistic Register and the Labor Bureau of the Middle West before she devoted herself to writing full time.

She received the NCTE Award for Excellence in Poetry for Children in 1978. She died in 2002.

"**P**oetry is a *required* taste. There are many children's books in my workroom. When my daughter Julia was ten she was thumbing through them in search of treasure. 'What's this one?' she asked, holding it up. 'That's verse,' I said. 'Yum,' said Jool, disappearing into a book. For Julia poetry is delicious, a required taste like milk and cookies. I couldn't agree with her more.

"Instead of building a fence of formality around poetry, I want to emphasize its accessibility, the sound, rhythm, humor, the inherent simplicity. Poetry can be as natural and effective a form of self-expression as singing or shouting." [4]

## You May Want to Know

Karla Kuskin was an artist as well as a poet; she illustrated most of the books she wrote. She designed the medallion for the NCTE Poetry Award; when she won it three years later (1979), her friends teased her and said, "Will you create other awards that you might win?"

Karla's student project became her first book, *Roar and More*. She created it in a graphics art course while working on her master's degree at the Yale School of Design.

Karla Kuskin was born on July 19, 1932, in New York City. She died in 2009.

"**I**n my creative-writing workshops and classes for young people, kindergarten through twelfth grade, and in my teaching at college level, I encourage students to approach their own writing and sharing of poetry with attention to established tradition and craft where needed, but to seek innovative patterns and language where they seem essential. It is in this way, I believe, that all of us grow." [5]

"What definition is there to encompass all the poems that have meaning and appeal to children? Do not definitions belong, rather, to science, to the laboratory? Our varying emotions, our needs as human beings, are not so easily stuffed into formulas and test tubes. The language of experience, of feeling, is not . . . the language of classification, and the point of poetry is not to arrive at a definition but to arrive at an experience—to feel, to bring our emotions and sensitivities into play." [6]

### You May Want to Know

Myra Cohn Livingston was born on August 17, 1926, in Omaha, Nebraska. She began writing poetry at age five; she later wrote plays and showed talent for music and sculpture. Myra's family moved from Omaha to Los Angeles when she was eleven years old; there she worked on the school newspaper. After graduating from Sarah Lawrence College, Myra returned to California.

She received the NCTE Award for Excellence in Poetry for Children in 1980. She died in 1996.

"**Y**ou may not 'get' all of a poem the first time you read it, because the words and the built-in music are so concentrated. Don't let it worry you; just go on to the end and then go back and read it again. You will find that the meaning begins to shine through. For a poem, with its rhythmic effects and use of word-pictures, has more than one level to explore. It becomes like a stone that you skim onto a lake; the ripples widen. New meanings unfold, and you have the pleasure of discovering more and more each time." [7]

## You May Want to Know

Eve Merriam was born in Philadelphia and graduated from the University of Pennsylvania. She did graduate work at the University of Wisconsin and Columbia University. After graduation from college, Eve worked as a sales clerk in a department store and as a fashion copywriter at *Glamour* magazine. She was also a playwright; several of her plays have been produced as Broadway and off-Broadway musicals. Eve lived in Greenwich Village, New York City, because she loved the rhythms and sounds of the city.

Eve won the NCTE Award for Excellence in Poetry for Children in 1981. She died in 1992.

"**I** dislike most of the children's poems I see because they seem written by a sponge dipped in warm milk and sprinkled with sugar. Children, as I know them from my own childhood and from my present parenthood, run to violent emotions. One of the best things children's poetry can do is to catch up that violence in the measure and play of rhyme, rhythm, and form—and so make a pleasant, if momentary, assurance of it." [8]

"Teachers can't say, 'Memorize . . . and give it back on demand. . . .' They are the ones who must entice the student. If a student can be brought to say 'Wow!' to one poem, he or she can say 'Wow!' to another. . . . Unless we lead students to this contact, Pac-Man is going to eat us all." [9]

**You May Want to Know**

John Ciardi was born on June 24, 1916, and taught at the University of Kansas City, Harvard University, and Rutgers University. He served as director of the Bread Loaf Writers' Conference at Middlebury College, received international acclaim for his translation of Dante's *Inferno*, served as poetry editor of the *Saturday Review*, served as host of the CBS show *Accent*, and wrote the classic textbook on poetry, *How Does a Poem Mean?* (1959). He received the Prix de Rome from the American Academy of Arts and Letters in 1956 and the NCTE Award for Excellence in Poetry for Children in 1982.

John Ciardi, the only son of Italian immigrants, graduated magna cum laude from Tufts University in 1938 and received his M.A. in English literature from the University of Michigan the following year. He died in 1986.

"**W**hen you hear a poem that sounds exactly right—when the words and the feelings seem inevitably to belong together—it is easy to believe that the poem, particularly if it is a poem for children—sprang full blown from the brow of the poet.

"Most of the poets I know work hard. The grain of sand that's supposed to irritate the creative center and produce a pearl often produces just the irritation. Lines that are supposed to dance sometimes drag their iambic feet. Words that were supposed to reflect light remain maddeningly dim. Or a cliché pops up that must be uprooted like a noxious weed. Then it's back to the typewriter, or the ball-point pen, or the pencil with a good eraser. And another wastebasket to fill." [10]

## You May Want to Know

Lilian Moore was born in New York City on March 17, 1909. She attended New York City schools, Hunter College, and did graduate work at Columbia University. She taught school in New York City and worked in a publishing house.

In 1985 she received the NCTE Award for Excellence in Poetry for Children. She died in 2004.

"Every day I go into my room and write.... Sometimes I write on yellow paper, writing and rewriting lots of drafts. A group of students who visited me at home called me 'the popcorn poet' because I fill my wastebasket with balls of crumpled up paper—drafts I reject." [11]

"I have made a concentrated effort to create a body of work: a family of young voices, through collections of my own poetry, that speak to, and through, the times of youth. My young people play sports and eat flying oatmeal cookies and search for interracial identities, and care about a solid hug." [12]

### You May Want to Know

Arnold Adoff has a love affair with food. Since he works at home, he is able to cook at the same time he is composing poems; he sometimes pauses from his work to stir the soup or punch down the bread dough. His passion for food is evident in his collections of poems *Eats*, *Chocolate Dreams*, and *Greens*.

Arnold Adoff was born on July 16, 1935, in the East Bronx section of New York City. He received his B.A. from City College and attended Columbia University and the New School for Social Research. He was a teacher in the New York City public schools in Harlem and the Upper West Side. He has taught at New York University and Connecticut College. He lives in Yellow Springs, Ohio.

He won the NCTE Award for Excellence in Poetry for Children in 1988.

"I write about what is vivid, exciting, magical to me—about the way I see things now, or how I viewed them as a child—or a combination of both child/adult feelings. I write about things that strike a chord in me, be it a lawnmower or a kaleidoscope or coat hangers. I have strong responses to what finds its way into my work.

"I would say write poetry for the fun of it, for the joy of it, for the love of it. And especially for the love of the things you write about, whatever they may be—whether beautiful or ugly, grand or humble, birds of paradise or mosquitoes, stars or mud puddles: All are worthy of being written about if you feel a deep affection for them—or, indeed, if you feel strongly about them in any way at all.

"It has always seemed to me that any tree or flower, any living creature, even any old board or brick or bottle possesses a mysterious poetry of its own, a poetry still wordless, formless, inaudible, but asking to be translated into words and images and sounds—to be expressed as a poem. . . . Poetry is simply a way of revealing and celebrating the essentially poetic nature of the world itself." [13]

**You May Want to Know**

Valerie Worth was born on October 29, 1933, in Philadelphia, Pennsylvania. Her father taught biology at Swarthmore College and joined The Rockefeller Foundation as a field biologist to study typhus. The family traveled to Bangalore, India, so her father could study malaria. Valerie attended one year of high school in Bangalore but later returned to Swarthmore for her bachelor of arts in English.

She received the NCTE Award for Excellence in Poetry for Children in 1991. She died in 1994.

"As a child growing up in Madison, Wisconsin, I read everything in sight, and drew pictures on anything that looked like it needed decoration. I wrote stories with my two best friends, and we all intended to be writers. We decided that I could always illustrate their books, in case my own efforts at writing didn't get me anywhere.

"When I was 14-and-a-half and in the 10th grade, my English teacher, Eulalie Beffel, looked at a poem I had written, and told me I was 'a writer.' When she introduced me to poets like Amy Lowell, Stephen Vincent Benét, and Emily Dickinson, she literally changed my life. Until then, I had not known that it was possible to use words in such exciting ways." [14]

"No matter what form my writing takes, I have tried to be as accurate with images of the natural world when I write poetry as I have had to be when writing books about the loon, the great horned owl, or the otter."

## You May Want to Know

Barbara Juster Esbensen was born in Madison, Wisconsin, in 1925 and spent the first twenty years of her life there. She graduated from the University of Wisconsin, majoring in art education. After receiving her degree, she taught art and creative writing to young adults on the tropical island of Truk in the Eastern Caroline Islands. Later, she taught third grade in Eureka, California.

She received the NCTE Award for Excellence in Poetry for Children in 1994. She died in 1996.

# Eloise Greenfield

"People-watching is not a hobby for me. It's a part of who I am and it always has been. I didn't notice that I was doing it when I was a child. But now, I remember. I can see myself watching the way people walked, talked, and stood, their facial expressions, and their gestures. I guessed at what they felt. Now, I use these impressions to create the characters in my poems and stories. I think the people-watcher was the writer in me, many years before I began to write."

## You May Want to Know

Eloise Greenfield was born on May 17, 1929, in Parmele, North Carolina. She recalls growing up in Langston Terrace, a public housing development for blacks in Washington, D.C. She and the other young residents in the housing project played games, danced in fire hydrant showers, and jumped rope. To her delight, the library was close by, and she visited often. Eloise was educated at Miner Teachers College, which trained black teachers in Washington, D.C. Her first job was as a clerk-typist in a government office. Her boredom from this job, however, allowed her time to begin her writing career. Greenfield took her inspiration from the fact that, at that time, there were far too few books that told the truth about African Americans. She has been writing children's books for almost thirty years. She is married to Robert Greenfield, and they have two children. [15]

Eloise Greenfield received the NCTE Award for Excellence in Poetry for Children in 1997.

"I guess that my writing for kids came about naturally. Not all poets like to rhyme anymore, or to write in rhythms, and I do. So, because kids like to hear the chime of words jingling together and like to feel the drumbeat of lines that bounce along, I've found very young people to be sympathetic readers and listeners. It's great fun to try to give them something they will like—and to hope that even adults, who were kids once, will like it, too."

**You May Want to Know**

X. J. Kennedy was born in Dover, New Jersey, on August 21, 1929. Irked by the hardship of having the name of Joseph Kennedy, he added an *X* and has been stuck with it ever since. At the age of twelve, Joe (as he is known) began his writing career and published his own science fiction magazine, *Terrifying Test-Tube Tales*. He went on to earn a B.A. degree at Seton Hall University, followed by his M.A. at Columbia University. Then he spent four years in the U.S. Navy, serving aboard destroyers as an enlisted journalist. Joe has also studied at the Sorbonne in Paris and the University of Michigan. He taught English at the University of North Carolina and moved to Tufts University in Massachusetts in 1963. He now lives in Lexington, Massachusetts, where he and his wife, Dorothy, have collaborated on four books. They have five children. [16]

X. J. Kennedy received the NCTE Award for Excellence in Poetry for Children in 2000.

# Mary Ann Hoberman

"I think of language as a vast treasury, free for the taking. I marvel that our forebears created this subtle and supple instrument, equally adapted to communicating the most routine transactions and the most inspired flights of imagination. Feeling this way about words, I approach them as unique individuals, each with its own family history, its own color and rhythm and sound, speaking to us out of the past, connecting us with our own pasts, trailing multiple meanings, many of them subliminal but there to be unearthed and made use of by the poet, the lover of language."

## You May Want to Know

Mary Ann Hoberman was born on August 12, 1930, in Stamford, Connecticut. She wrote for her school newspapers and edited her high school yearbook. In 1951 she earned a B.A. in history from Smith College and, thirty-five years later, an M.A. in English literature from Yale University.

Mary Ann has taught writing and literature to children as well as to college students. She cofounded and performed with The Pocket People, a children's theater group, and Women's Voices, a group that offers dramatized poetry readings. Since the publication of her first book, in 1957, her primary occupation has been writing for children.

Mary Ann married Norman Hoberman, an architect and artist, in 1951, and they've lived in Greenwich, Connecticut, for more than fifty years. They have four children, all of whom are involved in the arts, and five grandchildren. [17]

Mary Ann Hoberman received the NCTE Award for Excellence in Poetry for Children in 2003.

"**M**y childhood is, of course, a rich source of ideas. Apart from that, I'm a character-driven writer, and more often than not, my poems are dictated by the stories I wish to tell about my characters. In general, though, I find worthy subject matter everywhere I look. All that's required is that I be awake, alert, attentive to the people and events of my daily life."

**You May Want to Know**

Nikki Grimes grew up reading and loving books. Born in Harlem in 1950, she started writing when she was six and read her poems publicly for the first time at age thirteen. Her family was "troubled before I was added to it," and her parents repeatedly separated and reunited. Nikki and her sister were sent to live in foster homes. When Nikki was ten, she reunited with her family in Brooklyn. But in her neighborhood, gang fights were common, and she writes, "Some days, I wondered if I would survive."

She has gone back to many of these early experiences in writing her books for young adults. But Nikki says, "So far, none of my characters have been through half of what I have."

Although she had always done well in school, Nikki began to lose interest when her beloved father—her "best friend in all the world"—passed away when she was in high school. With the guidance of an English teacher, who was a Holocaust survivor, she regained her focus and concentrated on her schoolwork. She also met the writer James Baldwin, who mentored Nikki until she graduated from high school. From him, she "learned . . . to honor my talent, my gift. To write with honesty, integrity, and a sense of responsibility toward my audience." [18]

Nikki Grimes lives in Corona, California. She received the NCTE Award for Excellence in Poetry for Children in 2006.

"I still marvel when I finish writing a poem. I also continue to be thrilled each time I receive mail on *Been to Yesterdays: Poems of a Life*, a book that continues to be read after so many years and used in all kinds of programs from youth groups to AL-ANON. This story of a life of a child—me—who made it out of poverty has touched so many. While writing the book, I never would have known how the power of words could have such profound effect. At times poetry tells us we are not alone, we can reach out to one another with a few lines and, within a few lines, show we can strive for anything we reach for, go on toward tomorrows."

## You May Want to Know

Lee Bennett Hopkins was born in Scranton, Pennsylvania, in 1938. He grew up in a poor but close-knit family. As the oldest child, Lee had to help support his family, often missing school so he could work. He was an avid reader, enjoying everything from comic books and movie magazines to the occasional adult novel. Lee earned a bachelor's degree in education from Kean College and a master's degree from Bank Street College of Education. As a teacher, he used poetry in the classroom, launching his lifelong relationship with verse. In 1968, he joined Scholastic as an editor, a post he held until 1976, when he became a full-time writer and anthologist. His poetry collections cover a wide range of topics, including sports, geography, war, and holidays. He has written autobiographies, classroom materials, poetry books, and picture books as well as novels for young adults. Lee lives in Cape Coral, Florida.

Lee Bennett Hopkins received the NCTE Award for Excellence in Poetry for Children in 2009.

# Notes

1. Hopkins, Lee Bennett, *Pass the Poetry, Please!* (New York: HarperCollins, 1987), p. 107.

2. Hopkins, Lee Bennett, "Profile: Aileen Fisher," *Language Arts* (October 1978), Vol. 55, pp. 869, 871.

3. Fisher, Aileen, promotional material, Thomas Y. Crowell, 1978.

4. Kuskin, Karla, promotional material, HarperCollins, 1979.

5. Livingston, Myra Cohn, promotional material, McElderry Books, 1990.

6. Livingston, Myra Cohn, *Climb into the Bell Tower* (HarperCollins, 1990), p. 23.

7. Merriam, Eve, *What Can a Poem Do? An Explanation for Children and for Those Who Work with Children* (Atheneum, 1962), pp. 1–4.

8. Ciardi, John, *Something About the Author: Autobiography Series* (Detroit: Gale Research), p. 61.

9. Hopkins, Lee Bennett, *Pass the Poetry, Please!* (New York: HarperCollins, 1987), p. 13.

10. Koenig, Rachel, *Something About the Author*, Vol. 52 (Detroit: Gale Research), p. 129.

11. Adoff, Arnold, "Interview with Arnold Adoff," promotional material, Harcourt Brace, 1988.

12. Adoff, Arnold, "Politics, Poetry, and Teaching Children: A Personal Journey," *The Lion and the Unicorn*, 1986, Vol. 10, p. 9.

13. Hopkins, Lee Bennett, "Profile: Valerie Worth," *Language Arts*, (October 1991), Vol. 68, pp. 499–500.

14. HarperCollins promotional material.

15. African American Registry. www.aaregistry.com/detail.php?id=1933.

16. X. J. and Dorothy M. Kennedy. www.xjanddorothymkennedy.com.

17. Mary Ann Hoberman. www.maryannhoberman.com.

18. Annenberg Media. Teaching Multicultural Literature. www.learner.org/workshops/tml/workshop2/authors2.html.

# Bibliography

This bibliography is intended as a resource for further reading and highlights certain works by the poets. Many books are omitted due to space limitations.

## David McCord
*All Small: Poems by David McCord*. Illus. Madelaine Gill Linden. Little Brown, 1986.
*Away and Ago: Rhymes of the Never Was and Always Is*. Illus. Leslie Morrill. Little Brown, 1975.
*Every Time I Climb a Tree*. Illus. Marc Simont. Little Brown, 1967.
*One at a Time*. Illus. Henry B. Kane. Little Brown, 1986.
*The Star in the Pail*. Illus. Marc Simont. Little Brown, 1975.

## Aileen Fisher
*Always Wondering: Some Favorite Poems of Aileen Fisher*. Illus. Joan Sandin. HarperCollins, 1991.
*Anybody Home?* Illus. Susan Bonners. HarperCollins, 1980.
*The House of a Mouse*. Illus. Joan Sandin. HarperCollins, 1988.
*Like Nothing at All*. Illus. Leonard Weisgard. HarperCollins, 1979.
*Listen, Rabbit!* Illus. Symeon Shimin. HarperCollins, 1964.
*Out in the Dark and Daylight*. Illus. Gail Owens. HarperCollins, 1980.
*Rabbits, Rabbits*. Illus. Gail Niemann. HarperCollins, 1983.
*When It Comes to Bugs*. Illus. Chris and Bruce Degen. HarperCollins, 1986.

## Karla Kuskin
*Any Me I Want to Be*. HarperCollins, 1972.
*Dogs and Dragons, Trees and Dreams: A Collection of Poems*. HarperCollins, 1980.
*Herbert Hated Being Small*. Houghton Mifflin, 1979.
*Near the Window Tree: Poems and Notes*. HarperCollins, 1975.

## Myra Cohn Livingston
*Birthday Poems*. Illus. Margot Tomes. Holiday House, 1989.
*Celebrations*. Illus. Leonard Everett Fisher. Holiday House, 1985.
*Earth Songs*. Illus. Leonard Everett Fisher. Holiday House, 1986.
*Higgledy-Piggledy: Verses and Pictures*. Illus. Peter Sis. McElderry Books, 1986.

*I Like You, If You Like Me: Poems of Friendship*. McElderry Books, 1987.

*Space Songs*. Illus. Leonard Everett Fisher. Holiday House, 1988.

*There Was a Place and Other Poems*. McElderry Books, 1988.

*Up in the Air*. Illus. Leonard Everett Fisher. Holiday House, 1989.


## Eve Merriam

*Blackberry Ink*. Illus. Hans Wilhelm. Morrow, 1985.

*Chortles: New and Selected Wordplay Poems*. Illus. Sheila Hamanaka. Morrow, 1989.

*Fresh Paint*. Illus. David Frampton. Macmillan, 1986.

*It Doesn't Always Have to Rhyme*. Atheneum, 1964.

*Jamboree: Rhymes for All Times*. Illus. Walter Gaffney-Kessell. Dell, 1984.

*Poem for a Pickle: Funnybone Verses*. Illus. Sheila Hamanaka. Morrow, 1989.

*You Be Good and I'll Be Night: Jump-on-the-Bed Poems*. Illus. Karen Lee Schmidt. Morrow, 1988.


## John Ciardi

*Doodlesoup*. Illus. Merle Nacht. Houghton Mifflin, 1985.

*I Met a Man*. Illus. Robert Osborn. Houghton Mifflin, 1961.

*The Man Who Sang the Sillies*. Illus. Edward Gorey. HarperCollins, 1981.

*The Monster Den: or Look What Happened at My House—and to It*. Illus. Edward Gorey. Wordsong, 1991.

*The Reason for the Pelican*. Illus. Dominic Catalano. Wordsong, 1994.

*Someone Could Win a Polar Bear*. Illus. Edward Gorey. Wordsong, 1993.

*You Know Who*. Illus. Edward Gorey. Wordsong, 1991.

*You Read to Me, I'll Read to You*. Illus. Edward Gorey. HarperCollins, 1962.


## Lilian Moore

*I Feel the Same Way*. Illus. Robert Quackenbush. Macmillan, 1976.

*Something New Begins*. Illus. Mary J. Dunton. Macmillan, 1982.

*Think of Shadows*. Illus. Deborah Robison. Atheneum, 1980.

## Arnold Adoff

*All the Colors of the Race.* Illus. John Steptoe. Lothrop, 1982.
*Chocolate Dreams.* Illus. Turi MacCombie. Lothrop, 1989.
*Eats.* Illus. Susan Russo. Lothrop, 1979.
*Friend Dog.* Illus. Troy Howell. HarperCollins, 1980.
*Hard to Be Six.* Illus. Cheryl Hanna. Lothrop, 1991.
*In for Winter, Out for Spring.* Illus. Jerry Pinkney. Harcourt Brace, 1991.
*Sports Pages.* Illus. Steve Kuzma. HarperCollins, 1986.

## Valerie Worth

*All the Small Poems.* Illus. Natalie Babbitt. Farrar, Straus, 1987.
*More Small Poems.* Illus. Natalie Babbitt. Farrar, Straus, 1976.
*Small Poems.* Illus. Natalie Babbitt. Farrar, Straus, 1972.
*Small Poems Again.* Illus. Natalie Babbitt. Farrar, Straus, 1985.
*Still More Small Poems.* Illus. Natalie Babbitt. Farrar, Straus, 1978.

## Barbara Juster Esbensen

*Cold Stars and Fireflies: Poems of the Four Seasons.* Illus. Susan Bonners. HarperCollins, 1984.
*Swing Around the Sun.* Illus. Cheng-Khee Chee and others. Carolrhoda Books, 2003.
*Who Shrank My Grandmother's House? Poems of Discovery.* Illus. Eric Beddows. HarperCollins, 1992.
*Words with Wrinkled Knees: Animal Poems.* Illus. John Stadler. Wordsong, 1998.

## Eloise Greenfield

*Brothers and Sisters: Family Poems.* Illus. Jan Spivey Gilchrist. HarperCollins, 2009.
*Honey, I Love and Other Love Poems.* Illus. Diane and Leo Dillon. HarperTrophy, 1986.
*She Come Bringing Me That Little Baby Girl.* Illus. John Steptoe. HarperCollins, 1993.
*Under the Sunday Tree.* Illus. Amos Ferguson. HarperCollins, 1991.
*Water, Water.* Illus. Jan Spivey Gilchrist. HarperFestival, 1999.

## X. J. Kennedy

*The Forgetful Wishing Well.* Illus. Monica Incisa. McElderry Books, 1985.
*Ghastlies, Goops, and Pincushions: Nonsense Verse.* Illus. Ron Barrett. McElderry Books, 1989.
*The Kite That Braved Orchard Beach: Year-Round Poems for Young People.* Illus. Marian Young. McElderry Books, 1991.
*One Winter Night in August: And Other Nonsense Jingles.* Illus. by David McPhail. McElderry Books, 1975.
*The Phantom Ice Cream Man: More Nonsense Verse.* Illus. David McPhail. McElderry Books, 1979.

## Mary Ann Hoberman

*Fathers, Mothers, Sisters, Brothers: A Collection of Family Poems*. Illus. Marilyn Hafner. Joy Street Books, 1991.

*A House Is a House for Me*. Illus. Betty Fraser. Viking, 1978.

*The Llama Who Had No Pajama: 100 Favorite Poems*. Illus. Betty Fraser. Harcourt Brace, 1998.

*Yellow Butter, Purple Jelly, Red Jam, Black Bread*. Illus. Chaya Burstein. Viking, 1981.

*You Read to Me, I'll Read to You: Very Short Fairy Tales to Read Together*. Illus. Michael Emberley. Little, Brown, 2004.

## Nikki Grimes

*C Is for City*. Illus. Pat Cummings. Wordsong, 2002.

*Hopscotch Love: A Family Treasure of Love Poems*. Illus. Melodye Benson Rosales. Lothrop, 1999.

*It's Raining Laughter*. Photo. Myles C. Pinkney. Wordsong, 2005.

*My Man Blue*. Illus. Jerome Lagarrigue. Dial Books, 1999.

*What Is Goodbye?* Illus. Raúl Colón. Hyperion Books for Children, 2004.

## Lee Bennett Hopkins

*Alphathoughts: Alphabet Poems*. Illus. Marla Baggetta. Wordsong, 2003.

*Been to Yesterdays: Poems of a Life*. Illus. Charlene Rendeiro. Wordsong, 1995.

*City I Love*. Illus. Marcellus Hall. Abrams Books for Young Readers, 2009.

*Good Rhymes, Good Times*. Illus. Frané Lessac. HarperCollins, 1995.

*Sharing the Seasons* (anthology). Illus. David Diaz. McElderry Books, 2010.

# Permissions

Every possible effort has been made to trace the ownership of each poem included in *Another Jar of Tiny Stars*. If any errors or omissions have occurred, corrections will be made in subsequent printings, provided the publisher is notified of their existence.

Permission to reprint copyrighted poems is gratefully acknowledged to the following:

# Index

by AUTHOR, *Title*, and First line